This book is dedicated to Drenon.
He knows why.

Edited by Aileen Andres Sox
Designed by Dennis Ferree
Art by Kim Justinen
Typeset in 14/18 Weiss

ISBN: 0-8163-1181-1

94 95 96 97 98 • 5 4 3 2 1

No Puppy Food in the Garden

By Linda Porter Carlyle   Illustrated by Kim Justinen

Pacific Press Publishing Association
Boise, Idaho
Oshawa, Ontario, Canada

am swinging very slowly. I am sad. Mama is sad. Papa is sad too. Papa is sad because he won't be going to his office anymore. Mama says his office is "downsizing." I don't know just what that means except Papa can't work there anymore. Papa is out looking for a new job.

 am sad because Papa is sad. And I am sad because Mama is sad. And I am sad because Papa says I can't have a new puppy. "Not right now," he told me. "We can't afford to feed a puppy right now."

 am hungry. "Can I have an apple, Mama?"

"Sure," says Mama. "A red one or a green one?"

"Green, please," I say.

Mama washes a shiny green apple.

"Can we afford to feed me?" I ask.

Mama looks at me and smiles. "Of course, we can afford to feed you," she says. "We don't need to worry about running out of food. Our garden is growing nicely. We'll have plenty of potatoes and tomatoes and cucumbers and all the other things you like."

That's good," I say. "It's too bad we didn't plant any puppy food, though."

Mama looks at me and laughs. I laugh too. Mama thinks I'm funny.

an we afford to keep the new baby?" I ask. I wipe apple juice off my chin.

Mama looks down where her flat tummy used to be. It's all round and sticking out now because there is a baby inside her. She pats the place where the baby is. "Of course, we will keep the new baby!" she answers. She puts her arms around me and gives me a big hug. "The new baby is a special gift from God. God will provide for us so we can take care of the new baby. We will trust God."

hear Papa's car in the driveway. I run to see him.
"Hi, Papa! Do you have a new job?"

Papa looks tired, but he smiles at me and rumples my hair.
"No, not yet. No new job yet," he says.

am in bed, but I am not asleep. I hear soft voices in the dining room. I hear Mama and Papa talking. I know what they are talking about. They are talking about a new job for Papa. I am thinking about a new job for Papa. I am thinking about trusting God. Suddenly I have a question. I slide out of bed.

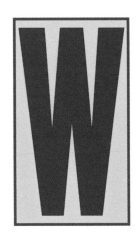

hat are you doing up?" asks Papa. "I think I remember tucking you into bed already."

I lean against Papa's chair. There are papers covered with numbers all over the dining-room table. Mama is working with the calculator. "Yes," she says, looking up. "I'm sure I remember tucking you into bed too."

"Even if we eat up all the food in the garden, and you don't have a new job, will we trust God?" I ask Papa.

apa looks at Mama. He scoots his chair back and lifts me up on his lap. "Yes," he says. "Even if we eat up all the food in the garden, and I don't have a new job, we will trust God. God knows what we need. He is our Father. He will take care of us."

I lean my head on Papa's shoulder. "God could send us food by ravens, like He did Elijah," I say. "But I've never seen a raven in our yard."

"I'm sure if God wants to send us food by ravens, He can find the ravens," Papa says.

f Elijah had a puppy, would the ravens have brought dog food?" I ask.

Papa chuckles softly. "I'm sure if Elijah had had a puppy, God would have provided for the puppy too.

nd I'm sure that when the time is right, God will provide a puppy for you."

"You need to get back in bed," says Mama.

jump off Papa's lap. "Good night," I say. "I love you."

Papa kisses the top of my head. "Mama and I love you. And God loves you too."

"I know," I say. I run to my room and snuggle down under my covers. I will think about puppy names and baby names before I go to sleep.

apa says God will take care of us. And Papa never tells me lies. So I know God will do it.

Parent's Guide

Share Your Faith With Your Child

A child's faith in God begins with faith in you, his parents. Here are some ideas to help you teach faith.

❖ Ask God to help you be a person whose word your child can trust—that you won't lie or make promises you don't keep. Thus you, by example, teach him that God also can be trusted.

❖ Remember that by meeting your child's needs, you teach her about God who supplies all our needs. Pray for help to discern what are "needs" and what are only "wants."

❖ Think of faith as a gift to nurture and protect. Ask God to help you deal with your own doubt and not to dwell on it, to voice your faith to your child and not create doubt in her mind. Read stories about people whose faith was strong even in terrible circumstances. Share family stories about how God has brought you through difficult times.

❖ Children sense trouble. If they don't know what is really wrong, they often will imagine that the problem is worse than it actually is, so it is best not to try to hide trouble from them. Explain the problem in terms they can understand. Share what you are doing to deal with the situation. Tell them something simple they can do to help. For example, if you are having financial trouble, tell them that Christmas or birthdays will have to be less elaborate. Ask them to help you think of ways to have fun as a family that don't cost a lot of money. Remember that your attitude toward difficulties can turn them into times that will knit your family closer together.

❖ When trouble comes, help your child look for evidences that God loves you even if He doesn't deliver you from a particular problem.

❖ Everybody has times when trouble seems to have arrived to stay and we cannot understand why. In those times, we need to go to God and ask Him to help us cling to Him in spite of circumstances. "Let us hold unswervingly to the hope we profess, for he who promised is faithful" (Hebrews 10:23, NIV).

Linda Porter Carlyle and Aileen Andres Sox

Books by Linda Porter Carlyle

I Can Choose
A Child's Steps to Jesus

God and Joseph and Me	*No Olives Tonight!*
Rescued From the River!	*Happy Birthday Tomorrow to Me!*
Grandma Stepped on Fred!	*No Puppy Food in the Garden*
Max Moves In	*Red and Purple on My Feet*
Cookies in the Mailbox	*Teddy's Terrible Tangle*
Beautiful Bones and Butterflies	*My Very, Very Best Friend*